Florence
Italy

City Map

 Glob:us

Florence, Italy — City Map
By Jason Patrick Bates

First Edition: October 2017

Scale / 1:4000

50m

500ft

Map Overview

Map Symbols

Highway		Map continuation page	
Street		Path	
Archaeological site		Kiosk	
Artwork		Level crossing	
Atm		Library	
Bar		Lighthouse	
Bicycle rental		Memorial	
Biergarten		Memorial plaque	
Buddhist temple		Monument	
Bus station		Museum	
Bus stop		Muslim mosque	
Cafe		Neighbourhood	
Camping site		Nightclub	
Car rental		Parking	
Cave entrance		Peak	
Chalet		Pharmacy	
Charging station		Picnic site	
Church / Monastery		Playground	
Cinema		Police	
Courthouse		Post office	
Department store		Prison	
Dog park		Pub	
Drinking water		Railway	
Dry cleaning		Restaurant	
Elevator		Shinto temple	
Embassy		Sikh temple	
Fast food		Sports centre	
Ferry terminal		Supermarket	
Fire station		Taoist temple	
Fountain		Taxi	
Fuel		Telephone	
Golf course		Theatre	
Guest house		Toilets	
Hindu temple		Townhall	
Hospital		Traffic signals	
Hostel		Viewpoint	
Hotel		Water park	
Information		Wilderness hut	
Jewish synagogue		Windmill	

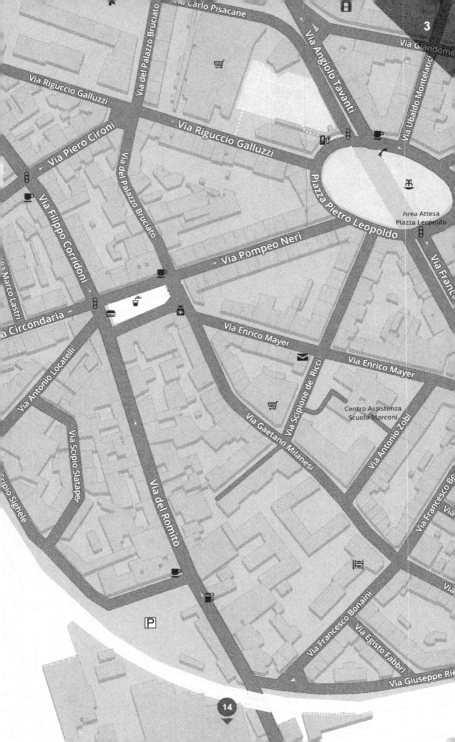

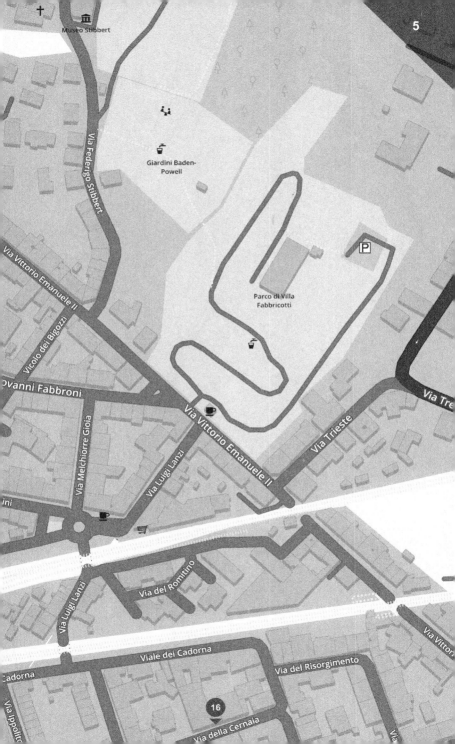

Museo Stibbert

Via Federigo Stibbert

Giardini Baden-Powell

Via Vittorio Emanuele II

Vicolo dei Bigozzi

Giovanni Fabbroni

Parco di Villa Fabbricotti

Via Melchiorre Gioia

Via Vittorio Emanuele II

Via Luigi Lanzi

Via Trieste

Via Tre

ini

Via Luigi Lanzi

Via del Romitino

Via Vittor

Viale dei Cadorna

Via del Risorgimento

Cadorna

Via della Cernaia

Via ippolit

Via

Via delle Forbici

parco del
ventaglio

20

Parco del
Ventaglio

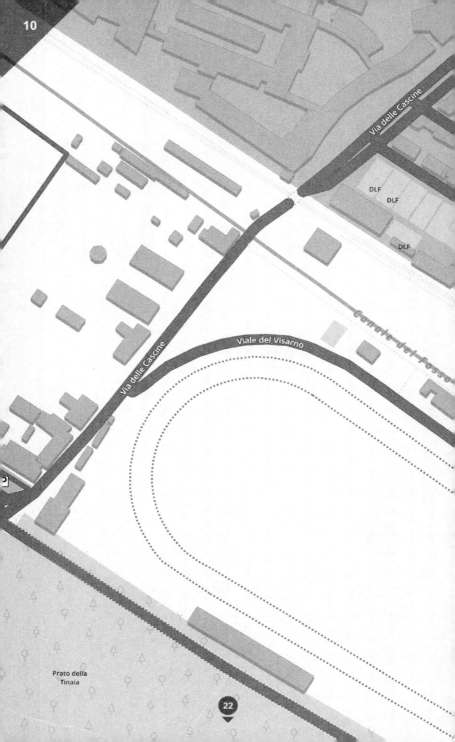

Via delle Cascine

DLF

DLF

DLF

Canale del fosso

Via delle Cascine

Viale del Visarno

Prato della
Tinaia

22

Piazza Giacomo Puccini

Via del Ponte alle Mosse

Via Gaetano Donizetti

Via Enrico Petrella

Via Ottavio Rinuccini

Via Giuseppe Saverio Mercadante

Via Amilcare Ponchielli

Via Giovanni Paisiello

Via Antonio

Viale del Visarno

23

Viale Francesco Redi

Via Filippo Pacini

Via Targioni Tozzetti

Via del Ponte all'Asse

Via Maragliano

ufficio postale

Via Maragliano

Via San Jacopino

Via Alfredo Catalani

Via Francesco Landini

Via Gaspare Luigi Spontini

Via Gioacchino Rossini

Via Domenico Cimarosa

Via Cassia

Via Benedetto Ma

Via Benedetto Marcello

Via Benedetto Marcello

Via Benedetto Marcello

Via delle Carra

Via Alessandro Scarlatti

Via Pierluigi da Palestrina

Via delle Carra

Via del Po

Via delle Port

Viale Belfiore

25

Ex Officine
Motori del
Romito

3

el Romito

Via del Romito

†

Via Crimea

Via Cosseria

Rivoluzione Ungherese
Via Caduti di Nassiriya

Via della

Viale Filippo Strozzi

Viale Belfiore

Piazzale Caduti nei Lager

Viale Francesco Redi

Viale Belfiore Via delle Ghiacciaie

Piazzale Montelungo

Via Cittadella

Via Guido Monaco

Via Iacopo Peri

Via delle Ghiacciaie

26

Via Antonio Ga

9

Via Antonio Meucci

Via Giovanni Aldini

Viale Alessandro Volta

Via Giovan Battist

Via Giovanni Inghirami

Via Giovanni Caselli

Via Luigi Galvani

Via Guglielmo Marconi

Via Nino Bixio

Via dei Cairoli

Via Pietro Carnesecchi

Via Aurelio

Via Goffredo Mameli

Viale dei Mille

Via Giovanni Duprè

Via Aurelio Saffi

Via San Gervasio

Via dei Sette Santi

Via Frusa

Via dei Sette Santi

Viale dei Mille

32

Via Antonio Cocchi

Via Augusto Baldesi

Via Augusto Baldesi

Via Leonardo Fibonacci

Istituto Nazionale
Ciechi

Teatro 13

Via Aurelio Nicolodi

Viale Ugo Bassi

Centro Assistenza
Scuola Carducci

Via Leonardo Fibonacci

Via Elbano Gasperi

Via delle Cento Stelle

Via San Gervasio

Via Volturno

Via Pastrengo

Viale Calatafimi

Viale Manfredo Fanti

Stadio Artemio
Franchi

Viale Maratona

Area Attesa
Campi di

33

P

le Abramo Lincoln

P

Via Baccio Bandinelli

Via del Franciabigio

Lungarno del Pignone

Arno

Via del Pignone

Via Baccio Bandinelli

Paolo Uccello
(Arno)

Via del Sansovino

Via del Pignoncino

Via del Rosso Fiorentino

Via de

Via Annibal Caro

34

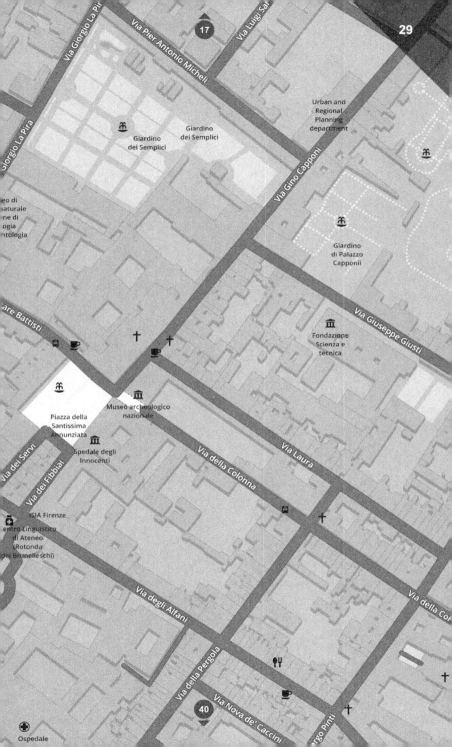

Via Giorgio La Pir

Via Giorgio La Pira

Via Pier Antonio Micheli

Via Luigi Sal

17

Urban and
Regional
Planning
department

Giardino
dei Semplici

Giardino
dei Semplici

Via Gino Capponi

Giardino
di Palazzo
Capponii

eo di
aturale
ne di
ogia
ntologia

are Battisti

Via Giuseppe Giusti

Fondazione
Scienza e
tecnica

†

†

Piazza della
Santissima
Annunziata

Museo archeologico
nazionale

Via Laura

Spedale degli
Innocenti

Via della Colonna

Via dei Servi

Via dei Fibbiai

ISIA Firenze

entro Linguistico
di Ateneo
(Rotonda
el Brunelleschi)

†

Via degli Alfani

Via della Co

Via della Pergola

⁜

Via Nova de' Caccini

40

rgo Pinti

†

Ospedale

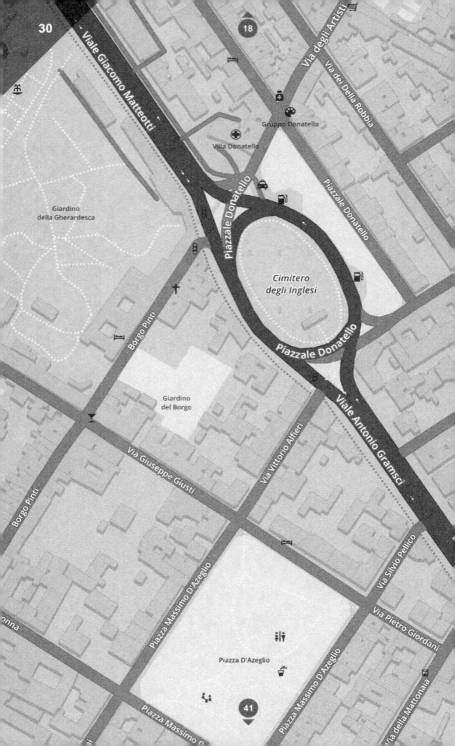

18

Viale Giacomo Matteotti

Via degli Artisti

Via dei Della Robbia

Gruppo Donatello

Villa Donatello

Giardino
della Gherardesca

Piazzale Donatello

Piazzale Donatello

Cimitero
degli Inglesi

Borgo Pinti

Piazzale Donatello

Viale Antonio Gramsci

Giardino
del Borgo

Via Giuseppe Giusti

Via Vittorio Alfieri

Via Silvio Pellico

Borgo Pinti

Via Pietro Giordani

onna

Piazza Massimo D'Azeglio

Piazza D'Azeglio

Piazza Massimo D'Azeglio

Via della Mattonaia

41

Piazza Massimo D

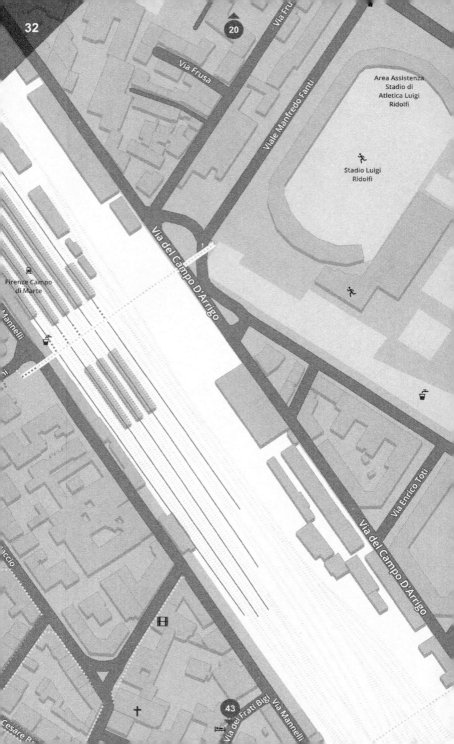

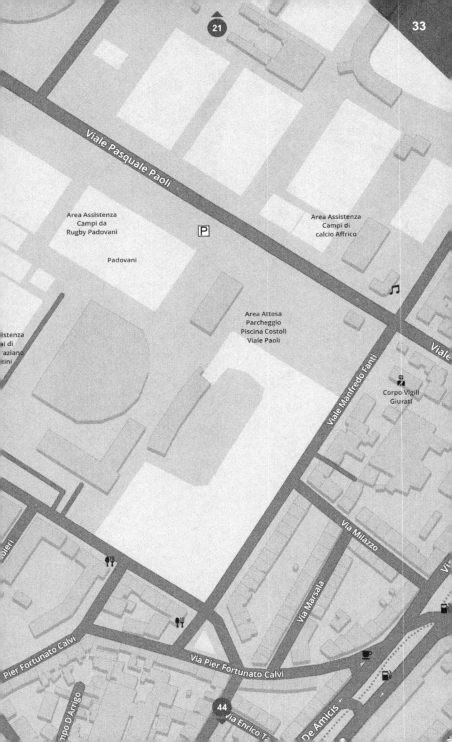

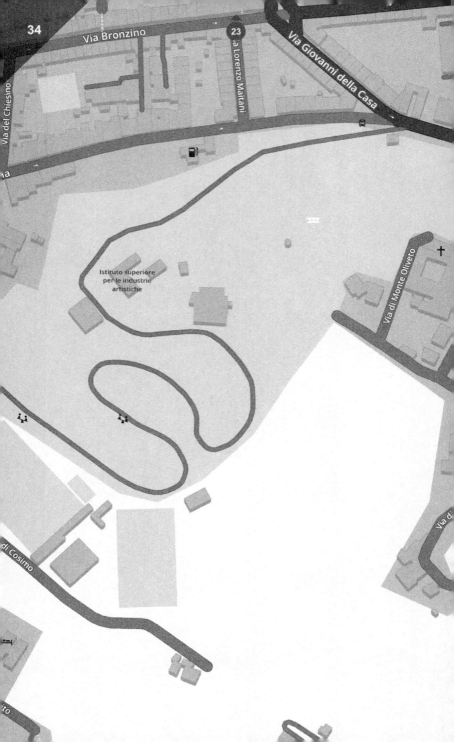

Via Bronzino

Via Lorenzo Maitani

Via Giovanni della Casa

Via del Chiesino

a

Istituto superiore
per le industrie
artistiche

Via di Monte Oliveto

Via di

di Cosimo

to

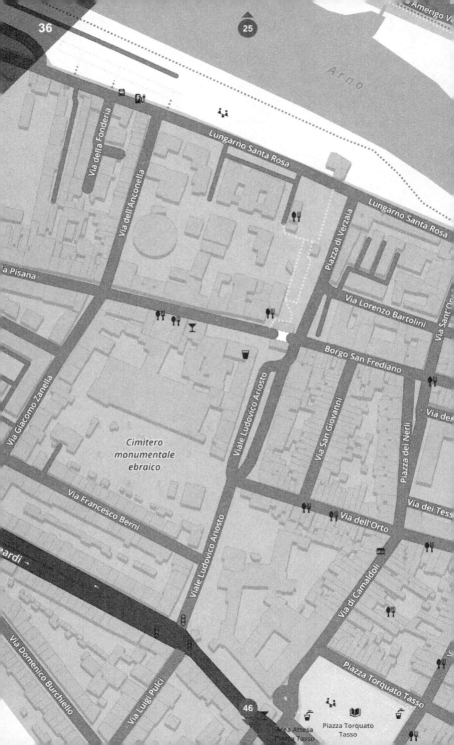

25

Arno

Via della Fonderia

Via dell'Anconella

a Pisana

Lungarno Santa Rosa

Lungarno Santa Rosa

Piazza di Verzaia

Via Lorenzo Bartolini

Via Sant'On

Via Giacomo Zanella

Borgo San Frediano

Via der

Cimitero
monumentale
ebraico

Viale Ludovico Ariosto

Via San Giovanni

Piazza dei Nerli

Via Francesco Berni

Via dell'Orto

Via dei Tess

ardi

Viale Ludovico Ariosto

Via di Camaldoli

Via Domenico Burchiello

Via Luigi Pulci

46

Piazza Torquato Tasso

Area Attesa
Piazza Tasso

Piazza Torquato
Tasso

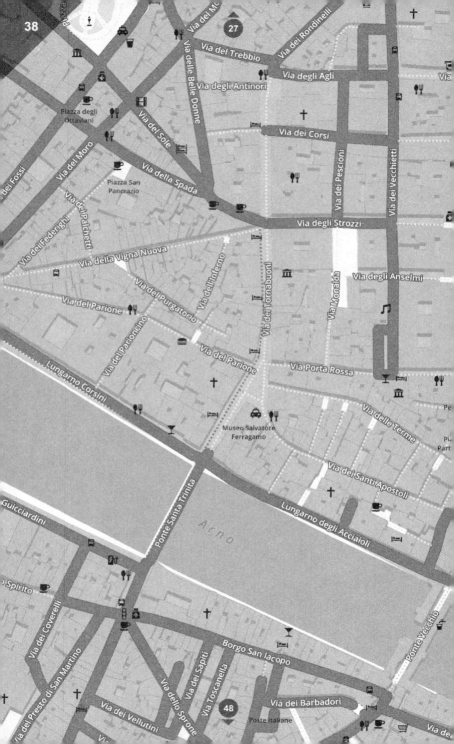

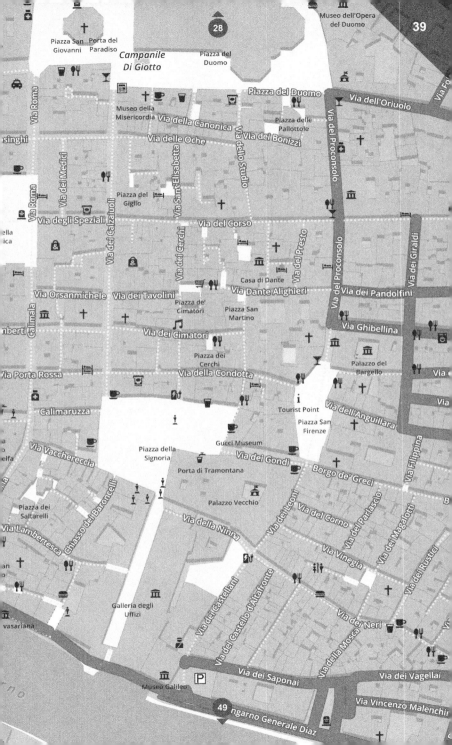

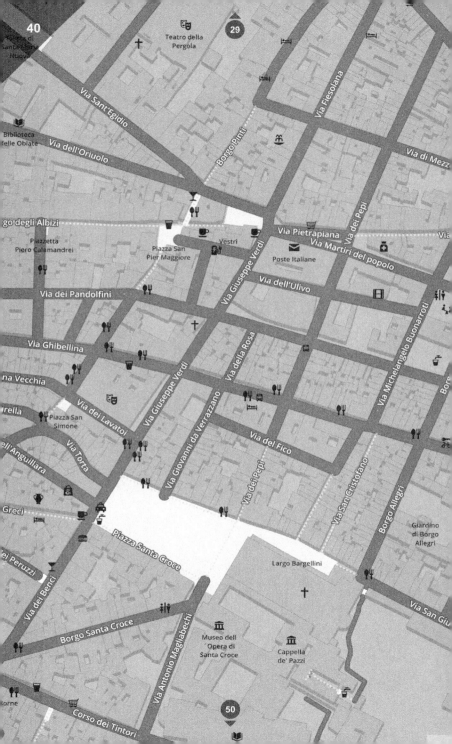

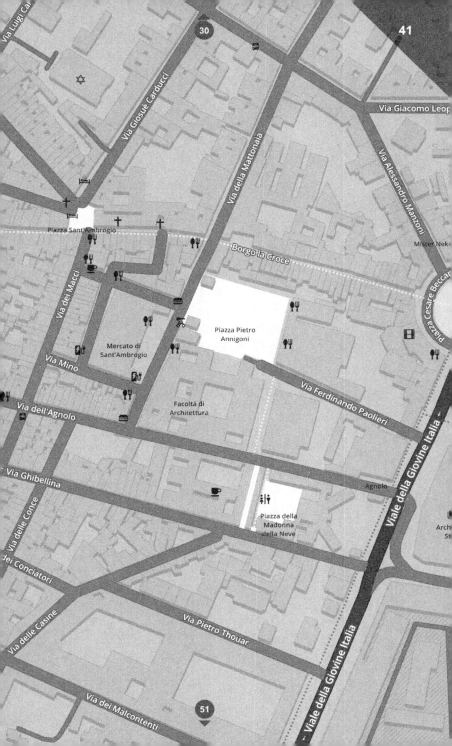

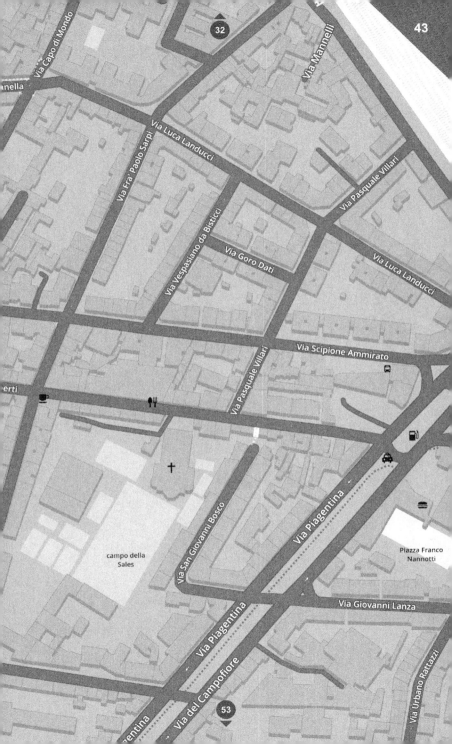

Via Capo di Mondo

nella

Via Mannelli

32

Via Fra Paolo Sarpi

Via Luca Landucci

Via Pasquale Villari

Via Vespasiano da Bisticci

Via Goro Dati

Via Luca Landucci

Via Scipione Ammirato

erti

Via Pasquale Villari

Via San Giovanni Bosco

Via Piagentina

campo della Sales

Piazza Franco Nannotti

Via Piagentina

Via Giovanni Lanza

Via del Campofiore

entina

Via Urbano Rattazzi

53

Via Andrea del Sarto

Via Adriano Mari

Via Aretina

Via Marco Minghetti

†

Impianto
sportivo Enio
Bartolini

Giardini di
Bellariva

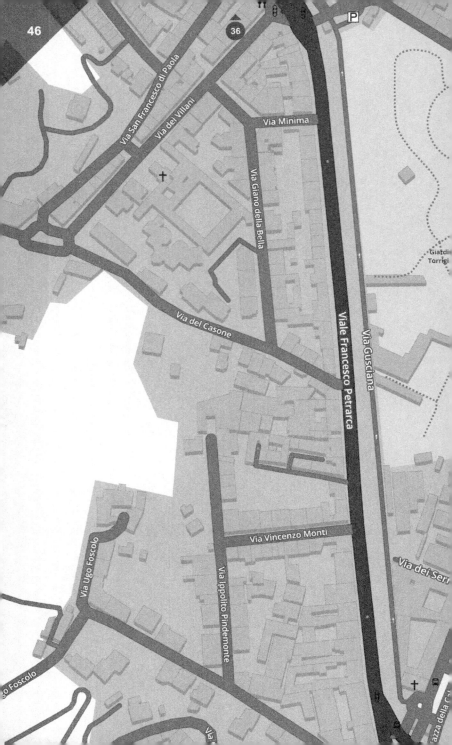

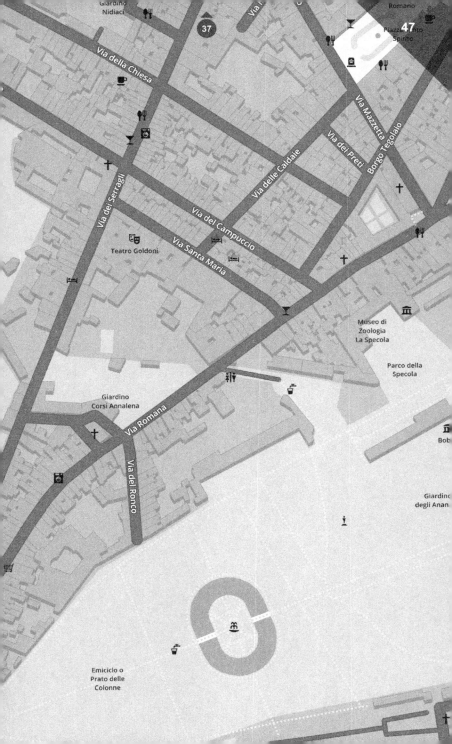

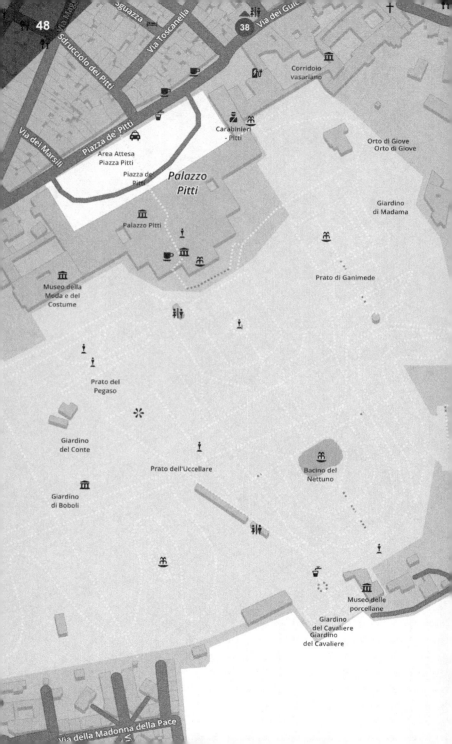

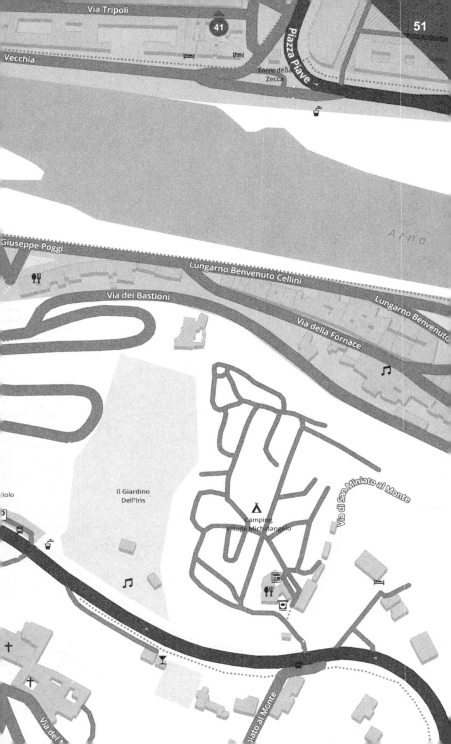

42

Lungarno del Tempio →

Lungarno de

Ponte San Niccolò

Giardino
Antonino
Caponnetto

Arno

Lungarn

Via Giampaolo Orsini

Via dei Baldovini

Via di Ricorboli

Via Ser Ventura Monachi

Via Carlo Marsuppini

Via Coluccio Salutati

Via dei Baldovini

P

Via Quintino Sella

43

Via Costantino Nigra

Via Urbano Rattazzi

gentina

Lungarno Cristoforo Colombo

Lungarno Cristofo

Arno

Ponte Gio

rrucci

Piazza Ravenna

Via Giampaolo Orsini

Via Coluccio Salutati

Via di Rusciano

Via Bartolon

Via di Ripoli

Streets

B

Borgo allegri 40, 41
Borgo degli albizi . 39, 40
Borgo dei greci . . . 39, 40
Borgo la croce 41
Borgo la noce 28
Borgo ognissanti . 26, 37
Borgo pinti 29, 30, 40
Borgo san frediano . . 36, 37
Borgo san iacopo 38
Borgo san lorenzo . . . 28
Borgo santa croce . . . 40
Borgo santi apostoli . . 38
Borgo stella 37
Borgo tegolaio . . . 47, 48

C

Calimala 39
Calimaruzza 39
Canto di croce rossa . 39
Cavalcavia dell'affrico 44
Cavalcavia delle cure 18
Chiasso altoviti 38
Chiasso borgherini . . . 38
Chiasso corneo 38
Chiasso cornino 38
Chiasso cozza 39
Chiasso degli altoviti . 38
Chiasso degli armagnati 39
Chiasso degli armati . 27
Chiasso dei baroncelli 39
Chiasso dei del bene . 38
Chiasso dei soldanieri 38
Chiasso del buco 39
Chiasso delle misure . 38
Chiasso di manetto . . 38, 39
Chiasso di san biagio . 38

Chiasso ricasoli 38
Chiasso san biagio . . . 38
Corso dei tintori . . 40, 50
Corso italia 24, 25, 36
Corso tintori 40
Costa al pozzo 49
Costa dei magnoli . . . 49
Costa del pozzo . . 38, 48
Costa san giorgio . 48, 49
Costa scarpuccia 49

L

Largo a.gennarelli 32
Largo adone zoli 6, 7, 17, 18
Largo alcide de gasperi 45
Largo alinari 27
Largo bargellini 40
Largo cesare cantù . . . 5
Largo fratelli alinari . . 27
Largo piero bargellini 40
Largo pietro annigoni 41
Lungarno aldo moro . 45
Lungarno amerigo vespucci . 24, 25, 36, 37
Lungarno benvenuto cellini 51, 52
Lungarno corsini . 37, 38
Lungarno cristoforo colombo 53
Lungarno degli acciaioli 38
Lungarno degli archibusieri 39
Lungarno dei pioppi . 22
Lungarno del pignone 22–24
Lungarno del tempio 52, 53

Lungarno della zecca vecchia 50, 51
Lungarno delle grazie 49, 50
Lungarno francesco ferrucci 52, 53
Lungarno generale diaz 39, 49
Lungarno guglielmo pecori giraldi . 51, 52
Lungarno guicciardini 37, 38
Lungarno santa rosa . 36
Lungarno serristori . . 49, 50
Lungarno soderini 36, 37
Lungarno torrigiani . . 39, 49

P

Piazza a. bonsanti 12
Piazza adua 27
Piazza antinori 38
Piazza augusto conti . 18, 30
Piazza bernardo tanucci 3
Piazza carlo goldoni . 37, 38
Piazza cesare beccaria 41, 42
Piazza d'ognissanti . . . 37
Piazza de' frescobaldi 38
Piazza degli adimari . 39
Piazza degli alberighi 39
Piazza degli ottaviani 38
Piazza degli scarlatti . 37
Piazza degli strozzi . . . 38
Piazza dei baroncelli . 39
Piazza dei bonsi 49
Piazza dei cavallari . . 38

Piazza dei cavalleggeri 50
Piazza dei cerchi 39
Piazza dei cimatori . . . 39
Piazza dei ciompi . 40, 41
Piazza dei davanzati . 38
Piazza dei donati 39
Piazza dei frescobaldi 38
Piazza dei giudici 39
Piazza dei giuochi 39
Piazza dei maccheroni 39
Piazza dei mozzi 49
Piazza dei nerli 36
Piazza dei pazzi . . 39, 40
Piazza dei peruzzi 39, 40
Piazza dei pesce . 38, 39
Piazza dei pitti 48
Piazza dei rossi . . . 38, 48
Piazza dei rucellai 38
Piazza dei salterelli . . 39
Piazza dei tigli 22
Piazza dei tre re 39
Piazza del capitolo . . . 39
Piazza del carmine . . . 37
Piazza del crocifisso . . 27
Piazza del duomo 28, 39
Piazza del giglio 39
Piazza del grano 39
Piazza del limbo 38
Piazza del mercato
    centrale 27, 28
Piazza del mercato
    nuovo 39
Piazza del pesce . 38, 39
Piazza del tiratoio 36, 37
Piazza delgi ottaviani 38
Piazza
    dell'indipendenza
    15, 16, 27, 28
Piazza dell'olio 39
Piazza dell'unità d'italia
    27
Piazza della calza 46
Piazza della costi-
    tuzione 15
Piazza della libertà . . . 17
Piazza della madonna
    della neve 41
Piazza della passera . 38
Piazza della repubblica
    38, 39
Piazza della santissima
    annunziata 29
Piazza della signoria . 39
Piazza della stazione 26,
    27

Piazza della vittoria 5, 16
Piazza delle belle arti 28
Piazza delle cure . . . 7, 18
Piazza delle murate . . 41
Piazza delle pallottole
    39
Piazza di cestello 37
Piazza di mercato
    nuovo 39
Piazza di parte guelfa 38
Piazza di san benedetto
    39
Piazza di san felice . . . 47
Piazza di san firenze . 39
Piazza di san francesco
    di paola 46
Piazza di san giovanni 39
Piazza di san lorenzo . 27
Piazza di san marco . . 29
Piazza di san martino 39
Piazza di san pancrazio
    38
Piazza di san paolino . 37
Piazza di san remigio 39
Piazza di san salvi 44
Piazza di san simone . 40
Piazza di santa cecilia 39
Piazza di santa croce 40
Piazza di santa felicita
    38
Piazza di santa maria in
    campo 39
Piazza di santa maria
    maggiore 38
Piazza di santa maria
    novella 27, 38
Piazza di santa maria
    nuova 39, 40
Piazza di santa trinita 38
Piazza di sta. maria al
    pignone 35
Piazza di verzaia 36
Piazza filippo baldinucci
    14
Piazza filippo
    brunelleschi 29
Piazza fra' girolamo
    savonarola 18
Piazza francesco fer-
    rucci 51,
    52
Piazza franco nannotti
    43
Piazza gaetano salvem-
    ini 40
Piazza galileo ferraris 20

Piazza giacomo puccini
    11
Piazza giampietro
    vieusseux 3, 4
Piazza giancarlo zoli . . 12
Piazza giorgini 4
Piazza giorgio vasari . 19
Piazza giovanni an-
    tonelli 21
Piazza giovanni rosadi
    45
Piazza giuseppe poggi
    50, 51
Piazza guglielmo ober-
    dan 42
Piazza isidoro del lungo
    17, 18
Piazza leon battista al-
    berti 43,
    44
Piazza leopoldo nobili
    20
Piazza lorenzo ghiberti
    41
Piazza ludovico antonio
    muratori 4
Piazza luigi dallapiccola
    12
Piazza madonna degli
    aldobrandini 27
Piazza massimo bo-
    gianckino 25
Piazza massimo
    d'azeglio 30, 41
Piazza mentana 39
Piazza nazario sauro . 37
Piazza nicola demidoff
    50
Piazza ognissanti 37
Piazza paolo uccello . 23
Piazza piattellina 37
Piazza piave 51
Piazza pier vettori . . . 35
Piazza piero poggi . . . 50
Piazza pietro annigoni 41
Piazza pietro leopoldo 3,
    4
Piazza pompeo batoni
    22
Piazza puliti 42
Piazza ravenna 53
Piazza san felice . . 47, 48
Piazza san giovanni . . 28
Piazza san iacopino . . 13
Piazza san lorenzo . . . 28
Piazza san marco . 28, 29
Piazza san paolino . . . 37

Piazza san pier mag-
    giore 40
Piazza sant'ambrogio . 41
Piazza santa caterina
    d'alessandria 16
Piazza santa elisabetta
    39
Piazza santa felicita . . 48
Piazza santa maria
    novella 27
Piazza santa maria so-
    prarno 49
Piazza santi gervasio e
    protasio 21
Piazza santo spirito . . 37,
    47
Piazza santo stefano . 39
Piazza taddeo gaddi . 24
Piazza thomas alva edi-
    son 21
Piazza torquato tasso 36,
    46
Piazza vittorio veneto 24,
    25
Piazzale bambine e
    bambini di beslan
    15
Piazzale caduti nei
    lager 14
Piazzale degli uffizi . . . 39
Piazzale delle cascine
    10
Piazzale di porta al
    prato 25
Piazzale di porta ro-
    mana 46,
    47
Piazzale donatello . . . 30
Piazzale michelangiolo
    50, 51
Piazzale montelungo 14,
    26
Piazzale oriana fallaci 15
Piazzale porta romana
    46
Piazzale thomas jeffer-
    son 23
Piazzetta dei del bene
    38
Piazzetta di san michele
    visdomini 28
Piazzetta piero cala-
    mandrei 40
Pista ciclabile arno sx
    49, 53
Pista ciclabile ferrucci
    51, 52

Pista ciclabile viali sud
    51, 52
Ponte a strisce 34
Ponte al pino 19
Ponte all'asse 13
Ponte alla carraia 37
Ponte alle grazie 49
Ponte alle riffe 8
Ponte amerigo vespucci
    36, 37
Ponte degli alpini 14
Ponte della vittoria . . . 24
Ponte dello statuto . . . 15
Ponte giovanni da ver-
    razzano 53
Ponte rosso 17
Ponte san niccolò 52
Ponte santa trinita . . . 38
Ponte vecchio 38
Pratello orsini 27

R

Rampa dei bastioni . . 51,
    52
Rampa dei canigiani . 48
Rampa delle coste . . . 49
Rampa di sotto 48

S

Sdrucciolo dei pitti . . . 48
Sottopasso fratelli
    rosselli 26

V

Via 20 settembre . 15–17
Via 24 maggio 15
Via 27 aprile 28
Via adriano mari 45
Via agnolo firenzuola . 7,
    8
Via agnolo poliziano . 16
Via agostino lapini 43, 44
Via alessandro levi 7
Via alessandro manzoni
    41
Via alessandro
    marchetti 19, 20
Via alessandro scarlatti
    13
Via alfonso la marmora
    17, 29
Via alfredo catalani . . . 13
Via alfredo oriani 4

Via amilcare ponchielli
    11, 12
Via andrea del
    castagno 19, 31
Via andrea del sarto . 44,
    45
Via andrea del verroc-
    chio 41
Via angelo m. bandini 3,
    4
Via angiolo tavanti 3
Via annibal caro . . 23, 34
Via anton f. doni . . . 11, 12
Via anton maria salvini 7,
    8
Via antonio cocchi 20, 21
Via antonio garbasso . 9,
    20
Via antonio genovesi . . 7
Via antonio giacomini 17,
    18
Via antonio locatelli . . . 3
Via antonio magliabechi
    40
Via antonio meucci . . 20
Via antonio pacinotti . 19
Via antonio scialoja . . 31,
    42
Via antonio squarcialupi
    11, 12
Via antonio stoppani . . 9,
    20
Via antonio vivaldi 12
Via antonio zobi 3
Via aretina 44, 45
Via arnolfo 42, 52, 53
Via attilio vallecchi . . . 19
Via attilio zuccagni or-
    landini 4
Via atto vannucci 4
Via augusto baldesi . . 21
Via augusto barazzuoli
    45
Via aurelio nicolodi . . . 21
Via aurelio saffi . . . 20, 21
Via baccio bandinelli
    22–24
Via baccio d'agnolo . . 22
Via barbacane 20
Via bartolommeo am-
    mannati 22
Via bartolommeo
    cristofori 13
Via bartolommeo scala
    53
Via benedetta 26
Via benedetto accolti 53

Via benedetto fortini . 52, 53
Via benedetto marcello 12–14
Via benedetto varchi 30, 31
Via benozzo gozzoli . . 35
Via bernardino ramazz- ini 33, 44
Via bernardino telesio 42
Via bernardo cennini . 27
Via bernardo rucellai . 26
Via bertoldo di giovanni 22, 23
Via bezzecca 6
Via bolognese 6, 17
Via bonifacio lupi . 16, 17
Via bonifazio lupi 16
Via borgognona 39
Via bronzino . . 23, 24, 34, 35
Via brunetto latini . . 8, 19
Via buffalmacco 8
Via c. nigra 53
Via caduti di nassiriya 14
Via calandrino 8
Via calimala 39
Via calzaiuoli 39
Via camillo cavour 17, 28, 29
Via campo d'arrigo . . . 44
Via capo di mondo . . 32, 42, 43
Via carlo botta 31, 42
Via carlo marsuppini . 52
Via carlo pisacane 3
Via carlo poma . . . 33, 44
Via cassia 13, 14
Via caterina franceschi ferrucci 45
Via cavour 28
Via celestino bianchi . . 4
Via cesare balbo . 31, 32, 43
Via cesare battisti 28, 29
Via cesare de laugier 18, 19
Via cesare guasti 4
Via chiara 27
Via cimabue 42
Via cino da pistoia . . 8, 9
Via circondaria 3
Via ciro menotti . . 31, 32, 42
Via cittadella . . 14, 25, 26

Via claudio monteverdi 12
Via coluccio salutati . 52, 53
Via cosimo ridolfi 15
Via cosseria 14, 15
Via costantino nigra . . 53
Via crimea 14
Via cristoforo landino 16
Via curtatone . 25, 26, 36
Via d'ardiglione . . . 37, 47
Via da' mori 47
Via damiano chiesa . . 33
Via daniele manin 31
Via dante alighieri 39
Via de amicis 44
Via de bardi 38
Via de' brunelleschi . . 38
Via de' cerretani . . 27, 28
Via de' ginori 28
Via de' neri 39
Via de' vagellai 39
Via de'cerretani 38
Via degli agli 38
Via degli alfani . . . 28, 29
Via degli anselmi 38
Via degli antinori 38
Via degli arazzieri 28
Via degli artisti 18, 19, 30
Via degli avelli 27
Via degli oleandri 22
Via degli orti oricellari 26
Via degli speziali 39
Via degli strozzi 38
Via dei baldovini 52
Via dei banchi 27, 38
Via dei barbadori 38
Via dei bardi . . 38, 39, 49
Via dei bastioni . . . 50–52
Via dei beccafumi 22
Via dei belfredelli 38
Via dei benci . 39, 40, 49
Via dei bentaccordi . 39, 40
Via dei biffi 28
Via dei boni 38
Via dei bonizzi 39
Via dei brunelleschi . . 38
Via dei bruni 6, 7
Via dei cairoli 20, 21
Via dei calzaioli 39
Via dei calzaiuoli 39
Via dei canacci 26
Via dei cappuccini 4
Via dei cardatori . . 36, 37
Via dei castellani 39
Via dei cavalieri 39

Via dei cerchi 39
Via dei cerretani . . 27, 28, 38, 39
Via dei cimatori 39
Via dei conciatori 41
Via dei conti 27, 38
Via dei corsi 38
Via dei coverelli 38
Via dei della robbia . . 18, 30, 31
Via dei federighi 38
Via dei fibbiai 29
Via dei fossi 37, 38
Via dei frati bigi . . . 32, 43
Via dei georgofili 39
Via dei geppi 37
Via dei giacomini 38
Via dei ginori 28
Via dei giraldi 39
Via dei girolami 39
Via dei gondi 39
Via dei gori 28
Via dei guicciardini . . 38, 48
Via dei lamberti . . 38, 39
Via dei lavatoi 40
Via dei leoni 39
Via dei ligustri 22
Via dei maccheroni . . 39
Via dei macci 40, 41
Via dei magalotti 39
Via dei magazzini 39
Via dei malcontenti . . 41, 51
Via dei marsili 48
Via dei martelli . . . 28, 39
Via dei martiri del popolo 40
Via dei medici 39
Via dei melograni 22
Via dei michelozzi 47, 48
Via dei mori 47
Via dei neri 39, 40
Via dei palchetti 38
Via dei pandolfini . 39, 40
Via dei pecori 38, 39
Via dei pepi 40
Via dei pescioni 38
Via dei pilastri . 29, 40, 41
Via dei preti 47
Via dei pucci 28
Via dei ramaglianti . . 38, 48
Via dei renai 49, 50
Via dei rondinelli 38
Via dei rustici 39

Via dei santi apostoli 38, 39
Via dei sapiti 38
Via dei saponai 39
Via dei sassetti 38
Via dei serragli 37, 46, 47
Via dei servi 28, 29
Via dei sette santi 19, 20
Via dei tavolini 39
Via dei tessitori 36
Via dei tornabuoni . . . 38
Via dei tosinghi . . . 38, 39
Via dei vagellai . . . 39, 40
Via dei vecchietti 38
Via dei velluti 38, 48
Via dei vellutini 38
Via dei villani 46
Via del baluardo 48
Via del bersaglio 7, 8
Via del biancospino . . 22
Via del campanile 39
Via del campidoglio . 38
Via del campo d'arrigo 19, 32, 33, 44
Via del campo di marte 33
Via del campofiore . . 43, 53
Via del campuccio . . 46, 47
Via del canneto 49
Via del canto alla quar-
    conia 39
Via del canto de' nelli 28
Via del canto dei nelli 27
Via del canto rivolto . 39, 40
Via del casone 46
Via del castellaccio . . 28, 29
Via del castello
    d'altafronte 39
Via del cestello 37
Via del chiesino 34
Via del corno 39
Via del corso 39
Via del crocifisso 40
Via del drago d'oro . . 36, 37
Via del fico 40
Via del fiordaliso 38
Via del forte di san gior-
    gio 49
Via del fosso macinante 24
Via del franciabigio . . 22, 23

Via del ghirlandaio . . 42, 43, 52
Via del giardino serris-
    tori 50
Via del giglio 27
Via del giuggiolo 6
Via del gomitolo
    dell'oro 27, 28
Via del lasca 8, 19
Via del leone 36, 37
Via del limbo 38
Via del madonnone . . 44
Via del melarancio . . 27
Via del mezzetta 45
Via del monte alle croci 50, 51
Via del moro . . 27, 37, 38
Via del muraglione . . . 45
Via del palazzo bruciato 3
Via del palazzo dei di-
    avoli 22
Via del pallone . . . 18, 19
Via del parioncino . . . 38
Via del parione . . . 37, 38
Via del parlagio 39
Via del parlascio 39
Via del passignano . . . 23
Via del pavone 38
Via del pellegrino . . . 6, 7
Via del piaggione 37
Via del pignoncino . . 23, 34
Via del pignone . . 23, 24
Via del ponte all'asse . 13
Via del ponte alle
    mosse 11–13, 25
Via del ponte alle riffe 7, 8
Via del ponte rosso . . . 17
Via del ponte sospeso 24, 35
Via del porcellana . . . 26, 27, 37
Via del pratellino 19
Via del pratello . . . 15, 27
Via del presto 39
Via del presto di san
    martino 38, 48
Via del proconsolo . . . 39
Via del purgatorio 38
Via del risorgimento . . . 5
Via del romitino 5
Via del romito 3, 14
Via del ronco 47
Via del rosso fiorentino 23, 34

Via del sansovino . 22, 23
Via del sole 38
Via del tiratoio 36, 37
Via del trebbio 38
Via del vanni 23, 24
Via del vetriciaio 12
Via dell'acqua 39
Via dell'agnolo . . . 40, 41
Via dell'albero 26
Via dell'alloro 27
Via dell'amorino 27
Via dell'anconella 36
Via dell'anguillara 39, 40
Via dell'ardiglione 37, 47
Via dell'ariento 27
Via dell'arte della lana 39
Via dell'erta canina . . 49, 50
Via dell'inferno 38
Via dell'isola delle
    stinche 40
Via dell'oche 39
Via dell'olmo 50
Via dell'orcagna . . 42, 52
Via dell'oriuolo . . . 39, 40
Via dell'orto 36, 37
Via dell'ortone 41
Via dell'osteria del
    guanto 39
Via dell'ulivo 40
Via della bellariva 44
Via della burella . . 39, 40
Via della canonica . . . 39
Via della cernaia 5, 15, 16
Via della chiesa . . 36, 37, 47
Via della colonna . 29, 30
Via della condotta . . . 39
Via della dogana . 28, 29
Via della fonderia 24, 35, 36
Via della fornace . 51, 52
Via della fortezza . 15, 27
Via della madonna
    della pace . . . 47, 48
Via della madonna
    della querce 8
Via della madonna
    della tosse . . . 17, 18
Via della mattonaia . 30, 41
Via della mosca 39
Via della ninna 39
Via della palancola 8
Via della pergola . 29, 40
Via della piazzola . . 8, 9

60

Via della piazzuola . . . 19
Via della rivoluzione
    ungherese 14
Via della rosa 40
Via della scala 25–27, 38
Via della spada 38
Via della stufa 28
Via della torre del gallo
    50
Via della torretta 44
Via della torricella . . . 45
Via della vigna nuova 38
Via della vigna vecchia
    39, 40
Via delle azalee 22
Via delle badesse 40
Via delle belle donne 27,
    38
Via delle bombarde . . 38
Via delle brache . 39, 40
Via delle burella . . 39, 40
Via delle caldaie 47
Via delle carra 13
Via delle cascine . . 10, 11
Via delle casine . . 40, 41,
    50, 51
Via delle cento stelle . 21
Via delle cerbine 8
Via delle cinque gior-
    nate 15
Via delle conce 41
Via delle farine 39
Via delle forbici 9, 19, 20
Via delle ghiacciaie . . 14,
    26
Via delle mantellate . 16,
    17
Via delle oche 39
Via delle pinzochere . 40
Via delle porte nuove 13,
    25
Via delle porte sante . 51
Via delle ruote 16, 28
Via delle seggiole . . . 40
Via delle terme . . . 38, 39
Via delle vecchie
    carceri 41
Via dello sprone . . 38, 48
Via dello statuto . . . 4, 15
Via dello studio 39
Via di barbano . . . 15, 27
Via di bellosguardo . . 46
Via di belvedere . . 49, 50
Via di camaldoli 36
Via di camporeggi . . . 16
Via di capaccio 39
Via di cestello 37

Via di mezzo 40, 41
Via di monte oliveto . 34,
    35
Via di montughi 5
Via di ricorboli 52
Via di ripoli 53
Via di rusciano 53
Via di san francesco di
    paola 36, 46
Via di san giuseppe . 40,
    41
Via di san iacopino . . . 13
Via di san leonardo . . 48,
    49
Via di san miniato al
    monte 50–52
Via di san miniato fra le
    torri 38, 39
Via di san niccolò 49, 50
Via di san paolino 37
Via di san pier maggiore
    40
Via di san salvatore al
    monte 50, 51
Via di san salvi 44
Via di san vito 34
Via di santa lucia 26
Via di santo spirito 37, 38
Via di serumido 47
Via dino compagni 8
Via dogali 19
Via domenico becca-
    fumi 22
Via domenico
    burchiello 35, 36, 46
Via domenico cimarosa
    13
Via domenico cirillo . . . 7
Via don giancarlo setti
    39
Via duca d'aosta . . 16, 17
Via edmondo de amicis
    33, 44
Via egisto fabbri 3
Via elbano gasperi . . . 21
Via elio gabbuggiani . 25
Via emanuele repetti . 31
Via enrico mayer 3
Via enrico petrella . 11, 12
Via enrico poggi . . 15, 16
Via enrico tazzoli . 33, 44
Via enrico toti 32
Via ermolao rubieri . . 32,
    33
Via ettore carafa 7
Via fabbroni 4
Via faentina 6–8, 17

Via faenza 27
Via fausto dionisi . . 15, 27
Via federigo stibbert . . 5
Via felice cavallotti . . . 35
Via felice fontana . 12, 13
Via ferdinando bar-
    tolommei 16
Via ferdinando paoletti
    4, 5
Via ferdinando paolieri
    41
Via ferdinando targetti
    44
Via ferdinando zannetti
    27, 28, 39
Via fiesolana 29, 40
Via filippina 39
Via filippo brunetti 8
Via filippo corridoni . . . 3
Via filippo pacini 13
Via fiume 27
Via folco portinari 39, 40
Via fra guittone 8
Via fra' bartolommeo 17,
    18
Via fra' domenico buon-
    vicini 18,
    19
Via fra' giovanni an-
    gelico 42,
    43
Via fra' iacopo passa-
    vanti 8, 18,
    19
Via fra' paolo sarpi . . . 43
Via fra' silvestro maruffi
    18
Via francesco berni . . 36
Via francesco bonaini . 3,
    4
Via francesco caracci-
    olo 8
Via francesco cilea . . . 13
Via francesco crispi . . . 4,
    15, 16
Via francesco
    d.guerrazzi . . . 30, 31
Via francesco da bar-
    berino 8
Via francesco de sanc-
    tis 44
Via francesco gianni 3, 4
Via francesco landini . 13
Via francesco marucelli
    4
Via francesco puccinotti
    5, 6, 15, 16

Via francesco rismondo 20
Via francesco valori . . 17, 18
Via francesco veracini 11
Via franco sacchetti . . . 7
Via fratelli bandiera . . 33, 44
Via fratelli bronzetti . . 21
Via fratelli dandolo . . . 44
Via fratelli poerio 7
Via fratelli ruffini 16
Via frusa 20, 32
Via gabriele d'annunzio 33
Via gabrio casati 44
Via gaetano donizetti . 11
Via gaetano milanesi3, 4
Via gaetano pilati 44
Via galliano 12
Via gaspare luigi spontini 12, 13
Via gaspero barbera . . 4
Via ghibellina 39–41
Via giacomo leopardi 41, 42
Via giacomo medici . 20, 21
Via giacomo zanella . 35, 36
Via giambattista vico 31, 32, 42
Via giambologna . 19, 30, 31
Via giampaolo orsini . 52, 53
Via gianbattista lulli . . 12
Via giandomenico romagnosi 3, 4
Via gianfrancesco pagnini 4
Via giano della bella . 46
Via gino capponi . 18, 29, 30
Via gioacchino rossini 13
Via giordano bruno . . 42
Via giorgio la pira 29
Via giosuè carducci . . 41
Via giotto 42, 43
Via giovan battista amici 20, 21
Via giovan battista fagiuoli 45
Via giovan battista niccolini 41

Via giovan battista zannoni 27
Via giovanni aldini . . . 20
Via giovanni antonio dosio 22
Via giovanni antonio sogliani . . 24, 35, 36
Via giovanni berchet . . 7, 18
Via giovanni boccaccio 7, 8
Via giovanni bovio 31, 42
Via giovanni caselli . . 20
Via giovanni da montorsoli 22
Via giovanni da verrazzano 40
Via giovanni della casa 34
Via giovanni duprè . . . 19, 20
Via giovanni fabbroni 3–5
Via giovanni fattori . . . 18
Via giovanni inghirami 20
Via giovanni lanza 43, 44
Via giovanni lorenzoni . 3
Via giovanni maria cecchi 52, 53
Via giovanni maria lampredi 4
Via giovanni michelucci 12, 24, 25
Via giovanni paisiello 10–12
Via giovanni pascoli . . 18
Via giovanni pico della mirandola 18
Via giovanni sercambi 7, 8
Via giovanni targioni tozzetti 13
Via girolamo benivieni 18
Via giulio cesare vanini 5, 16
Via giuseppe cesare abba 5, 16
Via giuseppe dolfi 15, 16
Via giuseppe galliano 11–13
Via giuseppe garibaldi 25
Via giuseppe giusti . . 29, 30

Via giuseppe la farina 30, 31
Via giuseppe montanelli 27
Via giuseppe richa . . 3, 4
Via giuseppe saverio mercadante . . 10–12
Via giuseppe tartini . . 10, 11
Via giuseppe verdi . . . 40
Via goffredo mameli . 20
Via goito 8
Via goro dati 43
Via guelfa 27, 28
Via guglielmo marconi 19–21
Via guglielmo massaia 4
Via guglielmo pepe . . . 7
Via guicciardini 48
Via guido cavalcanti . . 8, 19
Via guido guinizzelli . . . 8
Via guido monaco 14, 26
Via guido spadolini . . 14, 15
Via gusciana 46
Via gustavo modena . 17
Via iacopo da diacceto 25, 26
Via iacopo nardi . . 30, 31
Via iacopo peri 14
Via iacopo vignali 22
Via il prato 25, 26
Via ippolito nievo . . 5, 16
Via ippolito pindemonte 46
Via isola delle stinche 40
Via ix febbraio 5, 16
Via lambertesca 39
Via laura 29
Via leonardo bruni . . . 53
Via leonardo da vinci. 17, 18
Via leonardo fibonacci 21
Via leone x 16
Via lorenzo bartolini . . 36
Via lorenzo di credi . . 44
Via lorenzo il magnifico 15–17
Via lorenzo maitani . . . 34
Via luca giordano . 18, 19
Via luca landucci . 43, 44
Via luciano bausi . 12, 24, 25
Via luciano manara . . 44

Via lucrezia mazzanti 44
Via luigi alamanni 26
Via luigi boccherini . . . 11
Via luigi carlo farini . . 30,
    41
Via luigi einaudi 44
Via luigi galvani 20
Via luigi la vista 7
Via luigi lanzi 5
Via luigi passerini 4
Via luigi pulci 36, 46
Via luigi salvatore
    cherubini 17, 29
Via luigi settembrini . . . 7
Via luisa sanfelice 8
Via luna 42
Via lungo il mugnone . 7,
    18
Via lungo l'affrico . 33, 44
Via lupo 50
Via madonna della
    querce 8
Via madonna della
    tosse 17, 18
Via mafalda di savoia . 17
Via maffei 8, 9
Via maffia 37, 47
Via magenta 25
Via maggio . . . 38, 47, 48
Via mannelli . . 19, 31, 32,
    43, 44
Via maragliano 12, 13
Via marco lastri 3
Via marco minghetti . 44,
    45
Via marconi 20
Via mario pagano 7
Via marsala 33
Via marsilio ficino 18
Via martiri del popolo 40
Via masaccio . 18, 19, 31,
    32
Via maso finiguerra . . 26,
    37
Via matteo galdi 7
Via matteo palmieri . . 40
Via maurizio bufalini . 28,
    39, 40
Via mazzetta 47
Via melchiorre gioia . . . 5
Via melegnano 37
Via michelangelo
    buonarroti 40
Via micheli 29
Via milanesi 3
Via milazzo 33
Via minima 46

Via mino 41
Via monalda 38
Via montanara 18
Via montebello . . 25, 26,
    37
Via mortuli 22
Via mozza 39, 40
Via nardo di cione 42
Via nathan cassuto . . . 31
Via nazionale 27
Via nicola porpora 12
Via nino bixio 20
Via nova de' caccini . . 40
Via nove febbraio . . 5, 16
Via nuova dei caccini 29
Via onofrio zeffirini . . . 13
Via orazio dogliotti . . . 6
Via orsanmichele 39
Via ottaviano fabrizio
    mossotti 20
Via ottavio rinuccini . . 11
Via palazzuolo 26, 37, 38
Via palestro 25
Via panicale 27, 28
Via panzani 27, 38
Via paolo toscanelli . . 17
Via parioncino 38
Via pasquale villari . . . 43
Via pastrengo 21
Via pellicceria 38
Via piagentina 43, 53
Via pico della mirandola
    18
Via pier antonio micheli
    17, 29
Via pier capponi . . 17, 18,
    30
Via pier fortunato calvi
    33
Via pierluigi da palest-
    rina 13,
    25
Via piero cironi 3
Via piero di cosimo . . . 34
Via piero puccioni 32
Via pietrapiana . . . 40, 41
Via pietro carnesecchi
    20, 21
Via pietro colletta 42
Via pietro francavilla . 22
Via pietro giordani . . . 30
Via pietro jahier 6, 7
Via pietro maroncelli . 21
Via pietro metastasio 46
Via pietro thouar 41
Via pietro toselli . . 11–13
Via pippo spano 17

Via pisana 34–36
Via poggio bracciolini 53
Via pompeo neri 3
Via por santa maria . . 38,
    39
Via porta rossa . . . 38, 39
Via quintino sella . 44, 53
Via raffaello lambrus-
    chini 4,
    5
Via raffaello sanzio . . . 35
Via ricasoli 28
Via riguccio galluzzi . . . 3
Via roma 39
Via romana 46, 47
Via rosina 28
Via rosolino pilo . . 19, 20
Via sallustio bandini . 3, 4
Via salvestrina 17
Via san cristofano 40
Via san francesco di
    paola 36, 46
Via san gallo . . 16, 17, 28
Via san gervasio . . 20, 21
Via san giovanni 36
Via san giovanni bosco
    43
Via san giuseppe . 40, 41
Via san jacopino 13
Via san miniato 50
Via san miniato fra le
    torri 38, 39
Via san paolino 37
Via san pier maggiore
    40
Via san vito 34
Via san zanobi 16, 28
Via sandro botticelli . . 18
Via sant'agostino . 37, 47
Via sant'anna 17
Via sant'antonino . 27, 28
Via sant'egidio 40
Via sant'elisabetta . . . 39
Via sant'onofrio 36
Via sant'orsola 28
Via santa caterina
    d'alessandria 16
Via santa caterina da
    siena 26
Via santa margherita . 39
Via santa maria 47
Via santa monaca 37
Via santa reparata 16, 28
Via santa verdiana 41
Via santo spirito 37
Via scipio sighele 3
Via scipio slataper 3

Via scipione ammirato 42, 43
Via scipione de' ricci . . 3
Via ser ventura monachi 51, 52
Via sguazza 38, 48
Via sidney sonnino . . 44, 45
Via silvio pellico 30
Via silvio spaventa 17, 18
Via solferino 25
Via stefano türr 21
Via stracciatella 48
Via taddea 27, 28
Via targioni tozzetti . . . 13
Via teatina 38
Via timoteo bertelli 8, 19
Via tito speri 44
Via tommaso campanella 42, 43
Via torcicoda 22
Via tornabuoni 38
Via torta 40
Via toscanella 38, 48
Via trento 5, 6
Via trieste 5, 6
Via tripoli 50, 51
Via ubaldo montelatici 3
Via ugo foscolo 46
Via urbano rattazzi . . 43, 44, 53
Via v. malenchini 39
Via vacchereccia 39
Via val di lamona . 38, 39
Via valfonda 27
Via vasco pratolini 36, 46
Via venezia 17, 29
Via vespasiano da bisticci 43
Via vincenzio borghini . 7
Via vincenzo bellini . . . 12
Via vincenzo chiarugi 44
Via vincenzo gioberti 42, 43
Via vincenzo monti . . 46
Via vincenzo salvagnoli 16
Via vinegia 39
Via vittorio alfieri 30
Via vittorio emanuele ii 4-6, 17
Via vittorio fossombroni 31, 42
Via vittorio gui 12
Via volturno 21
Via zara 16, 17

Viale abramo lincoln 22-24
Viale aleardo aleardi 35, 36
Viale alessandro volta 7, 18-21
Viale antonio gramsci 30, 31, 42
Viale augusto righi . . . 21
Viale belfiore . . 13, 14, 25
Viale bernardo segni 30, 31
Viale calatafimi 21
Viale degli olmi 10, 22-24
Viale dei bambini 22
Viale dei cadorna . . 4, 5, 14, 15
Viale dei mille 18-20, 32
Viale del visarno . 10, 11, 23, 24
Viale della catena 22
Viale della giovine italia 41, 42, 51
Viale don minzoni . . 7, 17, 18
Viale duca degli abruzzi 41, 42
Viale edmondo de amicis 44
Viale enrico cialdini . . 33
Viale filippo strozzi . . . 14, 15, 26, 27
Viale francesco petrarca 46
Viale francesco redi . 13, 14
Viale francesco talenti 22
Viale fratelli rosselli . . 25, 26
Viale galileo 50
Viale giacomo matteotti 17, 18, 30
Viale giovanni amendola 42, 52
Viale giovanni lami . . 4, 5
Viale giovanni milton 15-17
Viale giuseppe mazzini 31, 32, 42
Viale giuseppe poggi 50, 51
Viale ludovico ariosto 36
Viale malta 32, 33
Viale manfredo fanti . 20, 21, 32, 33

Viale maratona . . . 21, 33
Viale michelangiolo . 51, 52
Viale pasquale paoli . 32, 33
Viale pierluigi nervi . . 21, 33
Viale raffaello sanzio . 35
Viale spartaco lavagnini 15-17
Viale stendhal 23
Viale ugo bassi 21
Viale vasco pratolini . 46
Vialetto amerigo gomez 45
Vialetto della piscina . 45
Vicolo degli adimari . . 39
Vicolo degli alberighi 39
Vicolo dei bigozzi 5
Vicolo dei cavallari . . 38, 39
Vicolo dei cerchi 39
Vicolo dei gondi 39
Vicolo dei malaspini . 39
Vicolo del barbi 6
Vicolo del bazar 39
Vicolo del canneto . . 48, 49
Vicolo del ferro 39
Vicolo del giappone . 38
Vicolo del giglio 39
Vicolo del panico 38, 39
Vicolo del tiratoio 36, 37
Vicolo dell'onestà 39
Vicolo dell'oro 38
Vicolo della cava 49
Vicolo della pergola . 29, 40
Vicolo della seta . 38, 39
Vicolo di ferro 39
Vicolo di san remigio 39
Vicolo di santa maria maggiore 38
Vicolo marzio 39
Vicolo san stefano . . . 38, 39
Vie dei maccheroni . . 39
Viuzzo dei bruni 6, 7
Viuzzo delle canne . . 42, 43
Viuzzo delle lane 18
Volta dei ciechi 39
Volta dei mazzucconi 39
Volta dei mercanti . . . 39
Volta dei tintori . . . 40, 50
Volta della vecchia . . 38
Volta di san piero 40

Points of Interest

A

Agricultural Institute (Via Cascine 11) 🏛 10

Arco di Trionfo in Piazza de la Liberta 👤 ..17

Art Gallery (Piazza de Pitti 1) 🏛 48

Art Museum Fondazione Romano (Piazza S.Spitito) 🏛 47

Auditorium-Former Church Santo Stefano al Ponte 👤 39

B

Ballerina Gardens 👤 .45

Baptistery St.John 👤 .39

Basicila and Piazza Santa Trinita 👤 .38

Basilica and Museum Santa Croce 👤 ..40

Basilica and Museum Santa Maria Novella 👤 27

Basilica San Lorenzo 👤 27, 28

Basilica Santo Spirito 👤 38

Batoni Light Rail Station 🚉 22

Bergallo Palace and Art Museum 🏛 39

Bigallo Museum (Piazza San Giovanni 1) 🏛 39

Boboli Gardens 👤 47, 48

Botanical Garden Semplici 👤 29

Bridge Alla Carraia 👤 37

Bridge Alle Grazie 👤 .49

Bridge Santa Trinita 👤 38

C

Cabinet of Drawings and Prints of the Uffizi (Via della Nina 5) 🏛 39

Campo di Marte Train Station 🚉 32

Cappelle Medicee (Piazza Madonna degli Aldobrandini) 🏛 27

Carabinieri Station (Viale Dei Mille 64) 🗡 19

Casa Buonarroti (Via Ghibellina 50) 🏛 40

Cathedral and Museum of Santa Maria del Fiore 👤 39

Cenacolo Andrea del Sarto 🏛 44

Cenacolo di Sant'Apollonia (Via 27 Aprile 1) 🏛 28

Central Library 👤 40

Chapel Pazzi 🏛 40

Chiostro Dello Scalzo (Cloister, Via Cavour 69) 🏛 28, 29

Church and Museum of Orsanmichele (Via Orsamichele) 🏛 .39

Church Madre della Divina Provvidenza 👤 8

Church of Saint Ambrose 👤 41

Church of San Michele degli Antinori 👤 .38

Church Oratorio Salesiano 👤 43

Church Sacred Heart 👤 14

Church Sacro Cuore 👤 32

Church San Bartolomeo A Monte 👤 34

Church San Felice (Via Mazzetta) 🏛 47

Church San Frediano in Cestello (Via de Cestello 4) 👤 37

Church San Giovanni Battista della Calza 👤 46

Church San Jacopino 👤 13

Church San Marco Vecchio 👤 7

Church San Michele and San Salvi 👤 .44

Church San Salvatore Al Monte 👤 51

Church Santa Margherita dei Cerchi (Via Corso 10) 👤 39

Church Santa Maria del Carmine 👤 37

Church SS Annunziata 👤 29

Church St. Bellariva 👤 45

Church St.James (Viale B.Rucellai 9) 👤 ..26

Church St.Salvatore In Ognissanti (Borgo Ognissanti) 👤 ...37

Comune di Firenze and Palazzo Vecchio (City Hall) 👤 39
Congress Palace (Piazza Adua 1) 👤 . . 27
Costoli Municipal Pool 🏃 33

E

Egyptian Museum (Via della Colonna 38) 🏛 29
English Cemetery 👤 . 30
EUI,Department of Economics - Villa San Paolo 🏛 8, 9
Evangelical Church Valdese (Via A.Micheli 26 and A.Marmora) 👤 . . . 17

F

Firenze Statuto Train Station 🚉 4
Forte di Belvedere 👤 48, 49
Fortezza da Basso (Ex-Fortress,Viale Filippo Strozzi 1) 👤 14, 15
Foundation of Science and Technology 🏛 29

G

Galleria Dell'Accademia (Via Ricasoli 58) 🏛 28
Gallery Rinaldo Carnielo 🏛 18
Gallery Uffizi 👤 39
Garden Dell'Iris 👤 51
Giotto's Bell Tower 👤 39
Gucci Museum 🏛 39

H

Hospital Santa Maria Nuova ✚ 29, 39
Hospital Villa Donatello ✚ 30

House of G.Galilei (Costa S.Giorgio 19) 👤 49
House-Museum of Dante 🏛 39

J

Jewish Cemetery 👤 . 36
Jewish Synagogue 👤 41

L

Le Cure Train Station (Via Luigi La Vista) 🚉 7
Light Rail Station Cascine 🚉 24
Light Rail Station Paolo Uccello 🚉 23
Limonaia Villa Strozzi (Via Pisana 77) 👤 34
Loggia dei Lanzi Open air Gallery (Piazza della Signoria) 👤 39
Loggia del Pesce (Piazza dei Ciompi) 👤 40, 41

M

Market Sant'Ambrogio 👤 41
Monument to Dante Alighieri in Piazza di Santa Croce 👤 40
Municipal Traffic Police HQ 🚓 25
Museum Alinari della Fotografia (Piazza S.Maria Novella 14) 🏛 38
Museum Bellini 🏛 37
Museum Casa Marteli (Via F.Zannetti 8) 🏛 27
Museum Casa Rodolfo Siviero 🏛 50
Museum Cenacolo di Fuligno 🏛 27
Museum Complesso San Firenze (Piazza San Firenze) 🏛 . 39
Museum Dell'Opificio Delle Pietre Dure

(Via degli Algfani 78) 🏛 28
Museum Galileo 🏛 . . . 39
Museum Horne (Via de Benci 6) 🏛 40
Museum Leonardo da Vinci (Via Cavour 21) 🏛 28
Museum Marino Marini (Piazza San Pancrazio) 🏛 38
Museum Misericordia (Piazza Duomo) 🏛 39
Museum Novecento (Piazza S.Maria Novella 10) 🏛 . . . 38
Museum of Anthropology (Via Proconsolo 12) 🏛 39
Museum of Fashion and Costume 🏛 48
Museum Of Natural History 🏛 29
Museum of Porcelain 🏛 48
Museum of Zoology La Specola 🏛 47
Museum S.Bardini (Via dei Renai 37) 🏛 . 49
Museum Salvatore Ferragamo 🏛 38
Museum Stibbert 🏛 . . . 5

N

National Archeological Museum 🏛 29
Nelson Mandela Forum (Piazza Berlinguer 2) 👤 33

O

Old Hospital of the Innocent 🏛 29

P

Palazzo alberti 👤 40
Palazzo Davanzati (Via Porta Rossa 13) 🏛 38
Palazzo di San Clemente (Via P.A.Micheli 2) 👤 29

Palazzo Pazzi (Via Pro-
consolo 10) 👤 . . . 39
Palazzo Pitti 🏛 48
Palazzo Strozzi 🏛 38
Panciatichi Palace (Via
Cavour 2) 👤 28
Paolo Graziosi Etr-
uscian Museum
(Via Sant'Edigio 21)
👤 40
Parish Immacolata e
San Martino 👤 4
Parish San Fran-
cisco (Piazza Fra
Girolano) 👤 18
Parish Santa Lucia Sul
Prato (Via di Santa
Lucia) 👤 26
Parish Santi Apostoli 👤
38
Parish Sette Santi
Fondatori 👤 20
Parish Sts.Gervasio and
Protasio 👤 21
Park Borgo Pinti 👤 . . . 30
Park Cascine 👤 . . . 22–24
Park Giardino
dell'Orticultura
👤 6
Park Villa Fabbricotti 👤 5
Park Villa Il Ventaglio 👤
9, 20
Park Villa Rusciano (Via
di Ripoli 70) 👤 . . . 53
Piazza Church and Mu-
seum San Marco 👤
28
Piazza de la Libertà 👤 17
Piazza Indipendenza
(Square) 👤 27
Piazzale Michalangelo
👤 50, 51
Polimoda International
Institute of Fashion
Design 🏛 25
Ponte Vecchio 👤 38
Porcellino Market
and Fountain (Pi-
azza del Mercato
Nuovo) 👤 39

Porta al Prato (Gate) 👤
25
Porta al Prato Train and
Light Rail Stations
🚆 25
Porta al Prato Train Sta-
tion 🚆 24
Porta alla Croce (Piazza
Cesare Beccaria) 👤
41, 42
Porta Romana (Piazza
della Calza) 👤 . . . 46
Porta San Frediano
(Borgo San Fre-
diano) 👤 36
Porta San Gallo (Gate)
👤 17
Porta San Giorgio (Via
Belvedere 35) 👤 49
Porta San Miniato (Via
San Miniato) 👤 . . 50
Puccini Theatre (Via
Cascine 41) 👤 . . . 10

Q

Questura-Police HQ 🛡
16, 17

R

Riccardi Medici Palace
(Via Cavour 3) 👤 28
Roman Amphitheatre 👤
40
Russian Orthodox
Church of the Na-
tivity (Via Leone X
8) 👤 16

S

San Lorenzo Market 👤
27
San Marco Vecchio
Train Station (Via
A.Levi) 🚆 7
Santa Maria Novella
Train Station 🚆 . 26

Spadolini Pavilion Ex-
hibition Center in
Basso Fortress 👤 15
Sports Complex
Cascine 🏃 24
St.Mark's English
Church (Via Maggio
16) 👤 38
Stadium Artemio
Franchi 🏃 20, 21, 33
Stadium Luigi Ridolfi 🏃
32
Statue of David and
Neptune Foun-
tain in Piazza de la
Signoria 👤 39

T

Theatre Maggio Musi-
cale Fiorentino 👤
24
Theatre Pergola 👤 . . . 40
Theatre Verdi 👤 40
Torre degli alberti 👤 . 40
Torre Della Zecca (Pi-
azza Piave) 👤 . . . 51
Torre San Niccolò 👤 . 50
Torrino di Santa Rosa
(Lugarno Santa
Rosa 2) 👤 36
Tourist Office (Piazza
della Stazione 4) 𝐢
27
Tourist Point Bigallo 𝐢
39

U

University of Florence
(Piazza San Marco)
🏛 28, 29

V

Vasari Corridor 👤 39
Visarno Arena Venue
and Hippodrome
🏃 10, 11, 22, 23

Printed in Great Britain
by Amazon

44818940R00040